Managerial Accounting

Exam Prep Guide

PEARSON

Prentice
Hall

Upper Saddle River, New Jersey
Columbus, Ohio

NATIONAL
RESTAURANT
ASSOCIATION

SOLUTIONS ™

DISCLAIMER:

The information presented in this publication is provided for informational purposes only and is not intended to provide legal advice or establish standards of reasonable behavior. Customers who develop food safety-related or operational policies and procedures are urged to obtain the advice and guidance of legal counsel. Although **National Restaurant Association Solutions, LLC (NRA Solutions)** endeavors to include accurate and current information compiled from sources believed to be reliable, **NRA Solutions**, and its **licensor, the National Restaurant Association Educational Foundation (NRAEF)**, distributors, and agents make no representations or warranties as to the accuracy, currency, or completeness of the information. No responsibility is assumed or implied by the NRAEF, NRA Solutions, distributors, or agents for any damage or loss resulting from inaccuracies or omissions or any actions taken or not taken based on the content of this publication.

Sample questions are designed to familiarize the student with format, length and style of the examination questions, and represent only a sampling of topic coverage. The performance level on sample questions does not guarantee passing of a ManageFirst Program examination. Further, the distribution of sample exam questions with their focus on particular areas of subject matter within a ManageFirst Competency Guide is not necessarily reflective of how the questions will be distributed across subject matter on the actual correlating ManageFirst exam.

Visit www.restaurant.org for information on other National Restaurant Association Solutions products and programs.

ManageFirst Program™, ServSafe®, and ServSafe Alcohol® are registered trademarks or trademarks of the National Restaurant Association Educational Foundation, used under license by National Restaurant Association Solutions, LLC a wholly owned subsidiary of the National Restaurant Association.

10 9 8 7 6 5 4 3 2
ISBN-13: 978-0-13-812691-9
ISBN-10:   0-13-812691-7

Contents

How to Take the
ManageFirst Examination

The ability to take tests effectively is a learned skill. There are specific things you can do to prepare yourself physically and mentally for an exam. This section helps you prepare and do your best on the ManageFirst Examination.

I. BEFORE THE EXAM

A. How to Study

Study the right material the right way. There is a lot of information and material in each course. How do you know what to study so you are prepared for the exam? This guide highlights what you need to know.

1. **Read the Introduction to each *Competency Guide*.** The beginning section of each guide explains the features and how it is organized.

2. **Look at how each chapter is organized and take clues from the book.**

   - *The text itself is important.* If the text is bold, large, or italicized you can be sure it is a key point that you should understand.

   - *The very first page tells you what you will learn.*

     Inside This Chapter: This tells you at a high level what will be covered in the chapter. Make sure you understand what each section covers. If you have studied the chapter but cannot explain what each section pertains to, you need to review that material.

Learning Objectives: After completing each chapter, you should be able to accomplish the specific goals and demonstrate what you have learned after reading the material. The practice exam as well as the actual exam questions relate to these learning objectives.

- *Quizzes and Tests*

  Test Your Knowledge: This is a pretest found at the beginning of each chapter to see how much you already know. Take this quiz to help you determine which areas you need to study and focus on.

- *Key Terms* are listed at the beginning of each chapter and set in bold the first time they are referred to in the chapter. These terms—new and specific to the topic or ones you are already familiar with—are key to understanding the chapter's content. When reviewing the material, look for the key terms you don't know or understand and review the corresponding paragraph.

- *Exhibits* visually depict key concepts and include charts, tables, photographs, and illustrations. As you review each chapter, find out how well you can explain the concepts illustrated in the exhibits.

- *Additional Exercises*

  Think About It sidebars are designed to provoke further thought and/or discussion and require understanding of the topics.

  Activity boxes are designed to check your understanding of the material and help you apply your knowledge. The activities relate to a learning objective.

- *Summary* reviews all the important concepts in the chapter and helps you retain and master the material.

3. **Attend Review Sessions or Study Groups**. Review sessions, if offered, cover material that will most likely be on the test. If separate review sessions are not offered, make sure you attend class the day before the exam. Usually, the instructor will review the material during this class. If you are a social learner, study with other students; discussing the topics with other students may help your comprehension and retention.

4. **Review the Practice Questions,** which are designed to help you prepare for the exam. Sample questions are designed to familiarize the student with the format, length, and style of the exam questions, and represent only a sampling of topic coverage on the final exam. The performance level on sample questions does not guarantee passing of a ManageFirst Program exam.

B. How to Prepare Physically and Mentally

Make sure you are ready to perform your best during the exam. Many students do everything wrong when preparing for an exam. They stay up all night, drink coffee to stay awake, or take sleep aids which leave them groggy and tired on test day.

There are practical things to do to be at your best. If you were an athlete preparing for a major event, what would you do to prepare yourself? You wouldn't want to compete after staying up all night or drinking lots of caffeine. The same holds true when competing with your brain!

1. **Get plenty of sleep.** Lack of sleep makes it difficult to focus and recall information. Some tips to help you get a good night's sleep are:

   - Make sure you have studied adequately enough days before the exam so that you do not need to cram and stay up late the night before the test.
   - Eat a good dinner the night before and a good breakfast the day of the exam.
   - Do not drink alcohol or highly-caffeinated drinks.
   - Exercise during the day, but not within four hours of bedtime.
   - Avoid taking sleep aids.

2. **Identify and control anxiety.** It is important to know the difference between actual test anxiety and anxiety caused by not being prepared.

Test anxiety is an actual physical reaction. If you know the information when you are **not** under pressure but feel physically sick and cannot recall information during the exam, you probably suffer from test anxiety. In this case, you may need to learn relaxation techniques or get some counseling. The key is how you react under pressure.

If you cannot recall information during reviews or the practice exam when you are not under pressure, you have not committed the information to memory and need to study more.

- Make sure you are as prepared as possible. (See "Anxiety Caused by Lack of Preparation")
- Take the exam with a positive attitude.
- Do not talk to other students who may be pessimistic or negative about the exam.
- Know what helps you relax and do it (chewing gum, doodling, breathing exercises).
- Make sure you understand the directions. Ask the instructor questions *before* the test begins.
- The instructor or proctor may only talk to you if you have defective materials or need to go to the restroom. They cannot discuss any questions.
- The instructor or proctor may continuously monitor the students so do not be nervous if they walk around the room.
- Know the skills described in Section II, During the Test.

3. **Anxiety Caused by Lack of Preparation.** The best way to control anxiety due to lack of preparation is focus on the exam. Whenever possible, you should know and do the following:

- Know the location of the exam and how to get there.
- Know if it is a paper-and-pencil test or an online exam. Pencils may be available but bring sufficient number 2 pencils if taking the paper-and-pencil version of the exam.
- If it is an online exam you may need your email address, if you have one, to receive results.
- You are prohibited from using purses, books, papers, pagers, cell phones, or other recording devices during the exam.
- Calculators and scratch paper may be used, if needed. Be sure your calculator is working properly and has fresh batteries.
- The exam is not a timed; however, it is usually completed in less than two hours.
- Take the sample exam so you know what format, style, and content to expect.
- Arrive early so you don't use valuable testing time to unpack.

II. DURING THE TEST

An intent of National Restaurant Association Solutions' ManageFirst exams is to make sure you have met certain learning objectives. If you are physically prepared, have studied the material, and taken the practice exam, you should find the ManageFirst exams to be very valid and fair. Remember, successful test taking is a skill. Understanding the different aspects of test preparation and exam taking will help ensure your best performance.

A. Test Taking Strategies

- Preview the exam for a quick overview of the length and questions.
- Do not leave any question unanswered.
- Answer the questions you are sure of first.

- Stop and check occasionally to make sure you are putting your answer in the correct place on the answer sheet. If you are taking an online exam, you will view one question at a time.
- Do not spend too much time on any one question. If you do not know the answer after reasonable consideration, move on and come back to it later.
- Make note of answers about which you are unsure so you can return to them.
- Review the exam at the end to check your answers and make sure all questions are answered.

B. Strategies for Answering Multiple-Choice Questions

Multiple-choice tests are objective. The correct answer is there, you just need to identify it.

- Try to answer the question before you look at the options.
- Use the process of elimination. Eliminate the answers you know are incorrect.
- Your first response is usually correct.

III. AFTER THE EXAM

Learn from each exam experience so you can do better on the next. If you did not perform on the exam as you expected, determine the reason. Was it due to lack of studying or preparation? Were you unable to control your test anxiety? Were you not focused enough because you were too tired? Identifying the reason allows you to spend more time on that aspect before your next exam. Use the information to improve on your next exam.

If you do not know the reason, you should schedule a meeting with the instructor. As all NRA Solutions ManageFirst exams are consistent, it is important to understand and improve your exam performance. If you cannot identify your problem areas, your errors will most likely be repeated on consecutive exams.

IV. EXAM DAY DETAILS

The information contained in this section will help ensure that you are able to take the exam on the scheduled test day and that you know what to expect and are comfortable about taking the exam.

- Have your photo identification available.
- Anyone with special needs must turn in an *Accommodation Request* to the instructor at least 10 days prior to the exam to receive approval and allow time for preparations. *If needs are not known 10 days prior, you may not be able to take the exam on the scheduled test day.*
- A bilingual English-native language dictionary may be used by anyone who speaks English as a second language. The dictionary will be inspected to make sure there are no notes or extra papers in it.
- If you are ill and must leave the room after the exam has begun you must turn in your materials to the instructor or proctor. If you are able to return, your materials will be returned to you and you may complete the exam. If it is an online exam you must close your browser and if the exam has not been graded yet, login in again when you return.
- Restroom breaks are allowed. Only one person may go at a time and all materials must be turned in prior to leaving the room and picked up when you return; or you must close your browser and login again for online exams.
- Make-up tests may be available if you are unable to take the exam on test day. Check with your instructor for details.
- If you are caught cheating you will not receive a score and must leave the exam location.

Managerial Accounting
Chapter Summaries and Objectives

Chapter 1 Managing Cash at the Operation

Summary

To properly manage a restaurant, there must be guidelines in place to ensure proper cash handling. Many operations already have their own procedures in place, and it is a manager's job to ensure staff are properly trained and procedures enforced.

It is critical to understand what goes into the accurate calculation of guest checks, including subtotals, sales tax, and gratuity. Tools such as tax tables and tip tables can make calculating by hand a quick process.

Each bill of U.S. currency has different security features that make the bill difficult for counterfeiters to duplicate. These features, such as watermarks, colored thread, and color-changing ink, vary by denomination. They provide a variety of ways to determine if bills are authentic. Change should always be given in the largest denominations possible. This can save time and improve accuracy, reducing the likelihood of counting errors.

Forms of non-cash payment include personal checks, credit cards, traveler's checks, and gift certificates. Each of these requires procedures for proper security and approval. Depending on the operation, some of these may not be accepted forms of payment.

Several guidelines should be in place to safeguard cash and receipts. Access to cash should be restricted, and should be stored securely at all times. Accurate counting and cash register reconciliation can reveal problems or mistakes.

A comparison is made to confirm that the money, checks, and credit card receipts in the register are equal to the recorded sales for a particular time period. This is called cash register reconciliation. Any variances between the report and the actual count should be noted and evaluated. Employees should be aware of what will happen if the drawer is over or short at the time of reconciliation. Whatever the over/short policy is, it should be followed consistently with each incident.

Preparing a bank deposit is the final step before removing money from the operation. Bank deposits should be made on a daily basis, and sometimes even more than once per day, depending on volume. Every bank deposit should be counted and verified by two people.

After completing this chapter, you should be able to:
- Describe best practices for monitoring cash handling at the operation.
- Calculate guest checks, including tax and tip amounts.
- Process cash and non-cash payments received from guests.
- Store cash and non-cash receipts securely.
- Perform cash register reconciliation.
- Prepare a bank deposit.

Chapter 2 Managing Payables and Receivables

Summary

A foodservice operation can be both customer and vendor on any given day. It is important to implement a system that makes the recording and processing of such transactions accurate and yet convenient.

Accounts payable is a term used to describe money the operation owes to others, such as suppliers of food, beverages, and other services. Such accounts need to be closely managed and monitored through the use of an established system. It is important to categorize payables using a chart of accounts so that the operation has an accurate, detailed history of its costs.

There are four basic steps to paying bills in an accurate manner. Every operation should have a system in place that ensures these payment-processing steps are followed consistently. Timely payment of accounts payable is also important, as many vendors give discounts for early payments. Prompt payment also ensures a good reputation with the supplier. A voucher system is one way to keep records of payments made to vendors.

Accounts receivable are those amounts due to the operation from others, usually customers and clients. In a restaurant operation, accounts receivable will most likely include house accounts and credit card accounts. Using a system to keep track of accounts receivable is as vital as it is for accounts payable.

Credit terms are the payment rules established for the account. These include such terms as how much credit is to be extended (credit limit) and when and how often payment is to be received, as well as any fees or penalties for a late payment.

The focus of an accounts receivable system should be to ensure that invoices are mailed out promptly and delinquent accounts are pursued. A good way to look at accounts receivable is to prepare an aging schedule showing the age of the accounts that are past due or outstanding.

After completing this chapter, you should be able to:
- Define accounts payable and describe a process for managing them.
- Define accounts receivable and describe a process for managing them.

Chapter 3 Exploring Costs

Summary

Costs can be classified in several ways. Cost categorization is used when preparing budgets, forecasting, and figuring break-even points.

One method of classifying costs in the foodservice industry is to categorize them as either controllable or noncontrollable costs. These are exactly what their names imply. Controllable costs are those costs that management can directly control. Examples include food costs over which management has little or no control. Examples include insurance and license fees.
In addition to controllable and noncontrollable, costs can also be expressed as either fixed, variable, or semivariable. This group of classifications is based on each cost's relationship to sales volume. Fixed costs remain the same regardless of sales volume. Insurance is an example. Variable costs go up and down as sales go up and down, and do so in direct proportion. An example is food costs. Semivariable costs are made up of both fixed costs and variable costs. An example of this is labor.

Some crossover is expected in classifying costs. Variable and semivariable costs are usually controllable. Fixed costs are typically noncontrollable. While there are some exceptions to this, for the most part it is true. Also, a particular cost can be classified differently depending on how it is budgeted.

After completing this chapter, you should be able to:
- Classify foodservice costs as controllable or noncontrollable.
- Describe and give examples of controllable and noncontrollable costs.
- Classify foodservice costs as variable, semivariable, or fixed.
- Describe and give examples of variable, semivariable, and fixed costs.

Chapter 4 Preparing the Operating Budget

Summary

An operating budget is a projected financial plan for a specific period of time. It lists the anticipated sales revenue and projected expenses, gives an estimate of the profit or loss for the period (often prepared for monthly time periods), and serves many purposes in the management of a foodservice operation. Most operating budgets are based on forecasts. A forecast is a prediction of sales levels or costs that will occur during a specific time period. The first step in creating an operating budget is forecasting anticipated sales revenue for the operation. Operational records such as sales histories, production sheets, and popularity indexes provide this information. Using the moving average technique, information for two or three recent and similar periods is averaged together. This averaging can produce a forecast that is more likely to be accurate, since it is not based solely on one period that might have been unique. There are several software products available to calculate sales forecasts.

Once there is a reliable forecast of sales revenue, management can move forward and forecast costs for the budget period. Past history is key to accurate cost forecasting as well. Managers should use any available records and tools to analyze historical cost data.

In general, the three categories of costs for a foodservice operation are food costs, labor costs, and other costs (also known as "overhead"). The key to forecasting food costs is to know the target food cost percentage. As long as you have a sales forecast and a target food cost percentage, the calculation of the forecasted food costs is straightforward.

Anticipated labor costs can be complicated to calculate. Fortunately, there is a step-by-step process that managers can follow. This process includes determining labor dollars available and distributing them among staff positions to create a schedule.

There are also a number of software programs available to assist managers.

Many of the other costs in a budget, such as rent or insurance, include fixed costs that will not change from period to period. Other costs, such as marketing, are determined by deciding what is needed and costing it out. These costs will vary and are usually specific to each operation. Again, historical records and POS reports help you determine these.

Once management has determined what income and costs are expected to be, they can compile the actual operating budget and estimate the expected profit or loss for the budget period.

After completing this chapter, you should be able to:
- Describe a foodservice operating budget.
- Forecast foodservice sales revenues and guest counts.
- Forecast foodservice operating costs.
- Prepare a master labor schedule for a foodservice operation.

Chapter 5 The Profit and Loss Report

Summary

In simple terms, a profit and loss report is a compilation of sales and cost information for a specific period of time. This report shows whether an operation has made or lost money during the time period covered by the report.

The profit and loss report, which is also called the income statement, is a valuable management tool. It helps managers gauge an operation's profitability as well as compares actual results to expected goals. Careful, periodic monitoring of this information – such as monthly or quarterly – helps management determine areas where adjustments must be made to bring business operations in line with established goals.

The profit and loss report lists sales income first. It then lists all expenses. The end of the report reflects the amount of profit or loss for the period covered. If sales are higher than costs, then the operation is making a profit. Conversely, if the total costs are higher than the total sales, the restaurant is running at a loss for the specified time period.

The first step in preparing a profit and loss report is to determine what time period the report should cover. Once that is decided, the financial records should be gathered. The next step is to figure out total sales for the period selected. Then, total costs, or expenses, need to be calculated for the same period. The profit or loss of a restaurant operation is simply the difference between the total sales (or income) and the total costs (or expenses).

Management looks carefully at profit and loss reports to determine the profitability of an operation, to judge the operation's efficiency, to determine where costs have gotten out of line, and to make basic management decisions.

There are several approaches to analyzing a profit and loss report. When a manager is comparing a recent profit and loss report to the budget, company standards, industry standards, or historical trends, he or she needs to be looking for any variances or changes that have occurred. This is a good way to check how the operation is running and can prevent future problems by catching them early. As soon as variances are observed, the manager should develop a plan of how to correct the problem.

After completing this chapter, you should be able to:
- Describe a profit and loss report, and explain its use.
- Prepare a profit and loss report based on sales and cost information.
- Analyze information found on a profit and loss report.

Chapter 6 Introduction to Cost Control

Summary

The process of controlling costs begins right where the budgeting process left off. Taking action to reduce operating costs depends on understanding which costs might be out of line and what can be done to correct them. With experience, managers quickly learn to quickly spot cost control concerns in their operations.

The relationship between sales and the costs that were incurred to achieve those actual sales is often proportional, and many foodservice costs change depending on sales volume. In order to know whether costs are in an appropriate range, it is imperative to start with accurate sales information. In addition to having accurate sales information, it is also necessary to have accurate cost information.

Once actual sales and costs are calculated, these figures are monitored and compared to budgeted amounts, operational standards, and historical information in order to identify any variances. This monitoring should be done on a regular and ongoing basis. This is a good way to check how the operation is running and can prevent future problems by catching them early. As soon as variances are observed, the manager should develop a plan of how to correct the problem. Over time, even small changes in costs can add up to significant losses or profits.

The two largest expenses in any foodservice operation are food cost and labor cost, and both can have an immediate impact on an operation's ability to make a profit. For this reason, managers must focus their efforts to keep these two costs under control.

There are several ways to evaluate food and labor costs. Food cost is often measured by comparing standards to actual food cost percentages. Waste and inventory productivity affect food cost as well. Performance and productivity ratios provide added details in order to perform accurate and meaningful labor cost analysis.

These ratios include labor cost percentage, sales per labor hour, average wage per hour, covers per hour, and sales per cover.

After completing this chapter, you should be able to:
- Explain the basic foodservice cost control process.
- Calculate food cost and food cost percentage.
- Analyze food product waste.
- Evaluate inventory performance and productivity.
- Calculate labor cost and labor cost percentage.
- Calculate labor productivity ratios, including sales per labor hour, average wage per hour, covers per hour, and sales per cover.

Chapter 7 The Capital Budget

Summary

Every operation has spending needs that fall outside of its daily costs of operation, such as improvements and upgrades. A capital budget is a spending plan for major purchases that will be used over a long period of time. Such expensive purchases, commonly known as furnishing, fixtures, and equipment (FF&E), are called capital items. A capital budget *does not include* day-to-day operating expenses.

To create a capital budget, you must first determine what capital needs exist. This results in a "wish list" of capital items, which you must then evaluate. Options for performing such analysis include analyzing costs and benefits for different options and comparing them, or calculating the payback period or the rate of return.

Then, you must prioritize and justify the need for each capital purchase. Assigning priorities helps you determine when to make the purchases, and in what order. Priority must be given to items that address a safety risk or ensure the operation meets local codes.

Since capital expenditures typically must be made over time, you must pre-plan when this spending will occur. This involves determining the priority or necessity of the project, as well as forecasting when funds for the projects will be available. Like any budget, capital budgets must be approved by the appropriate individuals in the operation.

After completing this chapter, you should be able to:
- Explain the purpose of a capital budget.
- Describe the process followed to prepare a capital budget.
- Assess an operation's capital needs.
- Evaluate different options for capital purchases.
- Prioritize and plan capital purchases.

Managerial Accounting Practice Questions

Please note the numbers in parentheses following each question. They represent the chapter and page number, respectively, where the content in found in the ManageFirst Competency Guide.

IMPORTANT: These sample questions are designed to familiarize the student with format, length and style of the examination questions, and represent only a sampling of topic coverage.

The grid below represents how the *actual* exam questions will be divided across content areas on the corresponding ManageFirst Program exam.

Managerial Accounting			
	1.	Managing Cash at the Operation	12
	2.	Managing Payables and Receivables	9
	3.	Exploring Costs	11
	4.	Preparing the Operating Budget	12
	5.	The Profit and Loss Report	17
	6.	Introduction to Cost Control	11
	7.	The Capital Budget	8
		Total No. of Questions	**80**

The performance level on sample questions does not guarantee passing of a ManageFirst Program examination. Further, the distribution of sample exam questions with their focus on particular areas of subject matter within a ManageFirst Competency Guide is not necessarily reflective of how the questions will be distributed across subject matter on the actual correlating ManageFirst exam.

1. What immediate items that should be considered when determining the current total costs for a restaurant? (5, 57)
   A. Invoices paid and payroll reports
   B. Unemployment rate and employee work schedules
   C. Pending menu labeling legislation and trans fat bans
   D. Economic trends and inflation

2. If sales should drop at a restaurant, payroll costs may need to be reduced in order to bring costs back in line. This would mean a reduction of hours. This is an example of which kind of cost? (3, 33)
   A. Fixed cost
   B. Variable cost
   C. Noncontrollable cost
   D. Controllable cost

3. What is calculated to find the subtotal? (1, 3)
   A. All gratuities for the server
   B. All the items ordered on a guest check
   C. Only the drinks ordered
   D. Only the food ordered

4. What is a method of calculating and recording the reduction in value of an asset over its useful lifetime? (4, 49)
   A. Depreciation
   B. Food cost
   C. Inflation
   D. Deflation

5. What is the term for money spent for employee wages, NOT including benefits? (6, 73)
   A. Payroll cost
   B. Labor cost
   C. Total cost
   D. Food cost

6. What term can be used to indicate if payment is received within 10 days of the invoice, a 2% discount will be received on the entire invoice? (2, 23)
   A. 2 or 10
   B. Due within 20 days
   C. 2/10
   D. Discount does not apply

7. Using the example of $20,000 cash outlay for a project and $5,000 net annual income for the project, what is the payback period? (7, 86)
   A. 4 years
   B. 2.5 years
   C. 3 years
   D. 5 years

8. What does bleeding a register mean? (1, 11)
   A. a new server takes over responsibility for the register
   B. money and credit card receipts are combined with those from other registers without counting
   C. extra cash is removed during restaurant operation to store cash more securely in a safe
   D. checks are placed beneath the register for safe keeping

9. What type of document is used by a vendor to list details such as items purchased, date of order, purchaser and sales price? (2, 21)
   A. Invoice
   B. Voucher
   C. Credit report
   D. Billing report

10. What is it called when a budget is checked against actual figures and the difference is noted? (6, 67)
    A. Corrective action
    B. Sales forecast
    C. Line item review
    D. Depreciation

11. What is a spending plan specifically for major purchases that will be used over a long period of time? (7, 82)
    A. Food budget
    B. Capital budget
    C. Time management
    D. Operating budget

12. What is a projected financial plan for a specific period of time? (4, 40)
    A. Cost estimate
    B. Sales forecast
    C. Operating budget
    D. Master plan

13. According to the Competency Guide, what is the largest reported fraud in the United States? (1, 9)
    A. Employee fraud
    B. Credit card fraud
    C. Embezzlement fraud
    D. Check fraud

14. What type of cost is made up of both fixed and variable costs? (3, 35)
    A. Fixed
    B. Variable
    C. Semivariable
    D. Noncontrollable

15. What is a direct financial comparison of cost/benefit analyses of two or more purchase options? (7, 86)
    A. Economy study
    B. Return on investment
    C. Payback period
    D. Operating budget

16. What is one technique used to help provide accurate sales forecasts in spite of fluctuations that may occur due to things such as severe weather? (4, 42)
    A. Weather trend
    B. Fluctuation method
    C. Average sales
    D. Moving average

17. When should variances be analyzed? (5, 59)
    A. On a quarterly basis
    B. When equipment orders are placed
    C. As soon as they are observed
    D. Once a year

18. What can be said of identifying and understanding costs? (3, 32)
    A. Helps managers interpret cost-related information and make financial decisions
    B. Is something only accountants need to understand
    C. Is too time consuming
    D. Helps employees understand customers

19. A manager observes a problem in that food waste has increased. To correct this problem, he better manages his food storage and rotation. What type of action did the manager take? (6, 69)
    A. Disciplinary action
    B. Forecasted sales revenue
    C. Corrective action
    D. Calculated payroll cost

20. What are known as capital items? (7, 83)
    A. Food products, consultant fees and labor costs
    B. Labor costs, delivery fees and taxes
    C. Furnishings, fixtures and equipment
    D. Employee meals, rent and seasonal help

21. According to the Competency Guide, it's recommended that how many people count the contents of a register drawer? (1, 12)
   A. One
   B. Two
   C. Three
   D. Four

22. What is the money a restaurant owes to others, such as a supplier of vegetables, called? (2, 20)
   A. Petty cash
   B. Accounts receivable
   C. Accounts payable
   D. Seed money

23. What is a measurement of how much food product is taken from inventory but not actually sold? (6, 72)
   A. Food stocked
   B. Food inventory surplus
   C. Food product waste
   D. Food total

24. When a chef changes a menu item so that it requires different ingredients, the amount and type of food items changes. This is an example of which type of cost? (3, 35)
   A. Noncontrollable
   B. Fixed
   C. Semivariable
   D. Variable

25. If sales are higher than costs, the operation is operating at a _____. (5, 58)
   A. loss
   B. profit
   C. trend state
   D. variance

26. Using the example of $5,000 income and $20,000 invested in the project, what is the rate of return? (7, 85)
    A. 41%
    B. 15%
    C. 25%
    D. 30%

27. What type of cost does not change regardless of how much income the restaurant receives? (3, 34)
    A. Fixed
    B. Variable
    C. Semivariable
    D. Controllable

28. What can state and local laws dictate? (1, 3)
    A. Amount of sales tax
    B. The gratuity that should be left
    C. The subtotal of the check
    D. Amount to charge for alcoholic beverages

29. What is a measurement of the relationship between sales and the expense spent on food in order to generate those sales? (4, 43)
    A. Food cost percentage
    B. Sales forecast
    C. Food cost forecast
    D. Operating budget

30. Using the example of $10,000 for food cost for one week and sales of $40,000, what would be the food cost percentage? (6, 71)
    A. 25%
    B. 20%
    C. 15%
    D. 27%

31. According to the Competency Guide, an operating budget serves many purposes in the management of a foodservice operation including what? (4, 41)
    A. Determining the hours of operation
    B. The amount of vacation time a manager should receive
    C. Outlining operating goals and managers' performance responsibilities
    D. Calculating retirement plans

32. According to the Competency Guide, why should payments that have been received be recorded, stored securely, and deposited as soon as possible? (2, 26)
    A. To allow money to start earning a return
    B. To ensure the manager does not forget about them
    C. To ensure the employees do not continue to bother the client by asking for payment
    D. To ensure good relationships with the client

33. What are the three essential steps in creating a capital budget? (7, 83)
    A. Assessing capital needs, evaluating identified needs, and prioritizing and justifying those needs
    B. Make a list of all the items wanted regardless of need, ask others for input on needs, and prioritize the list
    C. Put items on a list, place the list on the bulletin board, and ask employees to rate the items on the list
    D. Ask vendors what new equipment would be good for the operation, have customers provide input to what they would like to see added, and then prioritize the list

34. What is the formula most commonly used to determine sales forecast? (4, 41)
    A. (Number of customers) X (Average sales per customer)
    B. (Number of customers) X (Number of drinks purchased)
    C. (Average sales per customer) X (100)
    D. (Number of customers) X (100)

35. When should a manager usually bleed a register? (1, 11)
    A. At set times or after a busy sales rush
    B. When they need a break
    C. At the end of their shift
    D. When manager feels like doing it

36. What can a profit and loss report help managers do? (5, 56)
    A. Determine if and when the operation's building should be remodeled
    B. Determine customer satisfaction
    C. Gauge profitability and compare actual results to expected goals
    D. Prepare employee schedules

37. What is the term used to describe costs that management can directly control? (3, 32)
    A. Controllable costs
    B. Noncontrollable costs
    C. Fixed costs
    D. Variable costs

38. What is a list of categories used to organize an operation's expense information? (2, 21)
    A. Billing codes
    B. Item descriptions
    C. Chart of accounts
    D. Credit details

39. What is the formula for determining the dollars available for labor? (4, 44)
    A. (Payroll dollars available) – (fixed cost salaries)
    B. (Payroll dollars available) X (server payroll dollars)
    C. (Standard labor cost percentage) – (sales forecast)
    D. (Standard labor cost percentage) X (sales forecast)

40. Using the example of an employee who had $800 in sales and 40 covers, what would be the sales per cover for this employee? (6, 76)
   A. $10 per cover
   B. $12 per cover
   C. $15 per cover
   D. $20 per cover

41. What term is used to describe the measurement of the financial benefits of a purchase? (7, 84)
   A. Payback period
   B. Furnishings, fixtures, and equipment (FF&E)
   C. Return on investment (ROI)
   D. Rate of return

42. Profit and loss reports are useful when comparing what? (5, 60)
   A. Employee schedules
   B. What is actually occurring to what was budgeted
   C. Staff sick time
   D. One accountant to another accountant

43. What are payment rules established for accounts? (2, 24)
   A. Credit limits
   B. Amount owed
   C. Credit terms
   D. Balance

44. What is meant by covers per server? (4, 45)
   A. The number of servers working at a given time
   B. The number of managers working at a given time
   C. The number of meals a server can serve in an hour
   D. The number of employees a manager can manage at one time

45. What is the length of time it will take to recover the amount of an investment? (7, 86)
    A. Rate of return
    B. Payback period
    C. Return on investment
    D. Operating budget

46. What is the term used when every item on the budget is checked against actual figures and the differences are noted? (6, 67)
    A. Budget monitor
    B. Line item review
    C. Sales review
    D. Audit

47. According to the Competency Guide, when comparing a recent profit and loss report to the budget, company standards, industry standards, or historical trends, what does management need to be looking for? (5, 59)
    A. Overages
    B. Under runs
    C. Efficiency
    D. Variances

48. When a customer presents cash for payment, where the cash should be placed? (1, 7)
    A. In the register drawer before the change is counted
    B. In a visible spot until the change is counted and given to the guest
    C. Request the customer hold the payment until the cashier has change ready
    D. In a secure box in the manager's office

49. According to the Competency Guide, who usually approves
    payment of invoices? (2, 22)
    A. Any back-of-house employee who receives deliveries during
        scheduled delivery times
    B. A long standing employee who is well-liked by coworkers
    C. A vendor who gives the restaurant good discounts
    D. Someone who is aware of the overall budget and the current
        state of the finances

50. A manager's salary is $40,000 per year. A server's salary is $7.00
    per hour worked, but the schedule can vary from week to week.
    Both of these salaries are lumped into the category of labor costs.
    This is an example of which type of cost? (3, 35)
    A. Fixed
    B. Variable
    C. Semivariable
    D. Noncontrollable

Managerial Accounting
Answer Key to Practice Questions

1.	A		26.	C
2.	D		27.	A
3.	B		28.	A
4.	A		29.	A
5.	A		30.	A
6.	C		31.	C
7.	A		32.	A
8.	C		33.	A
9.	A		34.	A
10.	C		35.	A
11.	B		36.	C
12.	C		37.	A
13.	D		38.	C
14.	C		39.	D
15.	A		40.	D
16.	D		41.	C
17.	C		42.	B
18.	A		43.	C
19.	C		44.	C
20.	C		45.	B
21.	B		46.	B
22.	C		47.	D
23.	C		48.	B
24.	D		49.	D
25.	B		50.	C

Managerial Accounting Explanations to the Answers for the Practice Questions

Question #1
Answer A is correct. All costs should be included whether fixed or variable. Costs can be determined through either paper records or a POS system.
Answer B is wrong. It is difficult to place a value on the impact that unemployment rates have on a restaurant's current total costs.
Answer C is wrong. It is difficult to place a value on the impact of potential legislative concerns on a restaurant's total current total costs.
Answer D is wrong. It is difficult to place a value on the impact of economic trends and inflation when determining a restaurant's current total costs.

Question #2
Answer A is wrong. Fixed costs are cost that remain the same regardless of sales.
Answer B is wrong. Variable costs are costs such as the cost of food products required.
Answer C is wrong. Noncontrollable costs are items over which management has no control.
Answer D is correct. Costs associated with labor hours and rates are controllable by management.

Question #3
Answer A is wrong. Tax is added after the subtotal. Gratuity is only added in certain situations.
Answer B is correct. All of the items a customer ordered, both food and drinks, are added together to obtain the subtotal.
Answer C is wrong. Adding together only the drink items will not give the correct subtotal.
Answer D is wrong. Adding together only the food items will not give the correct subtotal.

Question #4

Answer A is correct. This accounting principle lets businesses make an expensive investment without showing a big loss at the time the investment is purchased.
Answer B is wrong. Food cost is not an expensive investment such as a piece of machinery and would not need to benefit from depreciation.
Answer C is wrong. Inflation is not related to reducing asset values.
Answer D is wrong. Deflation is not related to reducing asset values.

Question #5

Answer A is correct. Payroll cost only includes employee wages, both fixed and variable, but not employer's contribution to FICA and Medicare, workers' compensation insurance and employee benefits.
Answer B is wrong. Labor cost includes payroll cost as well as items such as FICA, Medicare, and workers' compensation.
Answer C is wrong. Total cost would include all costs, not just labor.
Answer D is wrong. Food cost is the cost of food, not labor.

Question #6

Answer A is wrong. This is not a valid accounting term.
Answer B is wrong. This does not state that a discount will be applied if paid within 20 days.
Answer C is correct. This term states that a 2% discount will apply if paid within 10 days. This practice is used to encourage prompt payment.
Answer D is wrong. This does not indicate that no discounts will apply.

Question #7

Answer A is correct. The formula is net cash outlay divided by annual income for the project. Using the example, $20,000 divided by $5,000 is 4.

Answer B is wrong. The formula is net cash outlay divided by annual income for the project. Using the example, $20,000 divided by $5,000 is 4.

Answer C is wrong. The formula is net cash outlay divided by annual income for the project. Using the example, $20,000 divided by $5,000 is 4.

Answer D is wrong. The formula is net cash outlay divided by annual income for the project. Using the example, $20,000 divided by $5,000 is 4.

Question #8

Answer A is wrong. If a cash register is not counted when servers change, you eliminate the responsibility of a server taking care to assure that their register is correct.

Answer B is wrong. Combining multiple registers does not make servers accountable for their own register.

Answer C is correct. Counting and securing the cash and credit card receipts helps to eliminate problems and secures the payments received.

Answer D is wrong. Placing checks beneath the register is not a secure method of handling the drawer contents.

Question #9

Answer A is correct. An invoice provides information regarding items received from an order.

Answer B is wrong. A voucher is used to record information about a payment.

Answer C is wrong. A credit report provides the status of a person's credit.

Answer D is wrong. A billing report provides information regarding overall billing.

Question #10

Answer A is wrong. Corrective actions can be taken after a budget is checked against actual figures.

Answer B is wrong. A sales forecast is a method for anticipating sales.

Answer C is correct. A line item review involves checking items on the budget against actual figures.

Answer D is wrong. Depreciation occurs when something loses value over time.

Question #11

Answer A is wrong. The food budget is for food items used daily and not for major expenses used over time.

Answer B is correct. Items purchased on a capital budget include furnishings, fixtures, and equipment.

Answer C is wrong. Time management does not affect the expenses.

Answer D is wrong. The operating budget is used for daily operations and not for long term major purchases.

Question #12

Answer A is wrong. A cost estimate provides information regarding products or services the restaurant may want to purchase.

Answer B is wrong. The sales forecast predicts the sales for a given period of time.

Answer C is correct. The operating budget lists the anticipated sales revenue and projected expenses and gives an estimate of the profit or loss for the period.

Answer D is wrong. A master plan is an operating plan and not a budget.

Question #13

Answer A is wrong. Employee fraud is not the largest reported fraud.

Answer B is wrong. Although there is a lot of credit card fraud, it is not the largest reported fraud.

Answer C is wrong. Embezlement fraud is not the largest reported fraud.

Answer D is correct. Check fraud is the largest reported fraud in the United States and involves billions of dollars.

Question #14

Answer A is wrong. Fixed costs remain the same regardless of sales volume.

Answer B is wrong. Variable costs go up and down in direct proportion to sales volumes.

Answer C is correct. Semivariable costs go up and down, but not in direct proportion to sales volumes.

Answer D is wrong. Noncontrollable costs are items over which management has no control.

Question #15

Answer A is correct. By comparing options management can determine what may be most economically advantageous to the operation.

Answer B is wrong. The return on investment is a measurement of the financial benefits of a purchase.

Answer C is wrong. The payback period is the length of time it will take to recover the cost of investment.

Answer D is wrong. The operating budget is used for daily operations and not for long term major purchases.

Question #16

Answer A is wrong. Although weather trends may affect sales, they are not used to calculate the sales forecast.

Answer B is wrong. Although fluctuation creates the need to look at data differently when calculating sales forecasts, this does not correctly define the technique used.

Answer C is wrong. While the method does average sales, it is important to be more specific about what is being averaged.

Answer D is correct. Sales information for two or three similar periods is averaged together to provide a forecast that is more accurate.

Question #17
Answer A is wrong. Variances should be analyzed as soon as they are observed.

Answer B is wrong. Variances should be analyzed as soon as they are observed, not when equipment orders are placed.

Answer C is correct. Variances should be analyzed as soon as they are observed so problems can be corrected.

Answer D is wrong. Variances should be analyzed and a plan of action determined as soon as they are observed.

Question #18
Answer A is correct. Managers need to understand the types of costs in order to make the good financial decisions.

Answer B is wrong. Not only accountants need to understand costs. Managers who make decisions about the operation need to understand costs.

Answer C is wrong. Understanding costs can be time consuming, but it is important to good management of the operation.

Answer D is wrong. Understanding costs has nothing to do with employees understanding customers.

Question #19
Answer A is wrong. Disciplinary action is not a common method for controlling food waste.

Answer B is wrong. Managing food storage and rotation has no direct connection to forecasting sales revenue.

Answer C is correct. The manager took action to correct a variance, the increase in food waste; therefore corrective action is the correct answer.

Answer D is wrong. Calculating payroll cost has nothing to do with food waste.

Question #20

Answer A is wrong. Food products are not capital items because they do not last beyond one year.

Answer B is wrong. Labor costs are not capital items.

Answer C is correct. Capital items are things such as furnishings, fixtures, and equipment. These are usually expensive items and the purchases are expected to last beyond one year.

Answer D is wrong. Employees meals, rent and seasonal help are not capital items as they are part of the operating budget.

Question #21

Answer A is wrong. Having only one person count the contents could lead to errors or theft.

Answer B is correct. When two people count the contents, there is less opportunity for error or theft.

Answer C is wrong. It is not necessary to have three people counting the contents of the drawer.

Answer D is wrong. Having four people counting the contents is not good time management.

Question #22

Answer A is wrong. Petty cash is small amounts of cash a business keeps on hand to pay for operating expenses that arise on an ongoing basis.

Answer B is wrong. Accounts receivable is money owed to the business by others.

Answer C is correct. Accounts payable is money the business owes vendors for goods or services they have received.

Answer D is wrong. Seed money is a term used for activities associated with starting a business.

Question #23

Answer A is wrong. Food stocked does not show how much food was taken and not used.

Answer B is wrong. Food inventory does not show how much food was wasted.

Answer C is correct. This figure includes costs for mistakes made during preparation, food that must be discarded, or food items that have been stolen or misused by staff.

Answer D is wrong. Food total is not a term used.

Question #24
Answer A is wrong. Noncontrollable costs are those costs over which no one has control. Changing a recipe or menu item is controllable.
Answer B is wrong. Food costs are variable, not fixed.
Answer C is wrong. Food items are variable, not semivariable.
Answer D is correct. Food items are variable costs and are controllable.

Question #25
Answer A is wrong. When costs are higher than sales, the result is a loss.
Answer B is correct. When sales are higher than costs, the result is a profit.
Answer C is wrong. This is not a valid term.
Answer D is wrong. Variance is not a term used to define profit or loss.

Question #26
Answer A is wrong. The formula is income divided by the amount invested in the project. Using the example, $5,000 divided by $20,000 is 25%.
Answer B is wrong. The formula is income divided by the amount invested in the project. Using the example, $5,000 divided by $20,000 is 25%.
Answer C is correct. The formula is income divided by the amount invested in the project. Using the example, $5,000 divided by $20,000 is 25%.
Answer D is wrong. The formula is income divided by the amount invested in the project. Using the example, $5,000 divided by $20,000 is 25%.

Question #27
Answer A is correct. Fixed costs are costs that remain the same regardless of sales volume.
Answer B is wrong. Variable costs go up and down in direct proportion to sales volumes.
Answer C is wrong. Semivariable costs go up and down as sales go up and down.
Answer D is wrong. Controllable costs are costs management can control.

Question #28
Answer A is correct. Percentages used to determine sales tax are governed by state and local laws.
Answer B is wrong. Gratuity percentages are determined by the customer.
Answer C is wrong. The subtotal is determined by adding the drink and food items.
Answer D is wrong. State and local laws do not determine the amount to charge for alcoholic beverages.

Question #29
Answer A is correct. The key to forecasting food cost is to know the desired, or target, food cost percentage.
Answer B is wrong. The sales forecast is used along with the food cost percentage to calculate the food cost forecast.
Answer C is wrong. The food cost forecast is calculated using the sales forecast and the food cost percentage.
Answer D is wrong. The operating budget is a projected financial plan.

Question #30
Answer A is correct. The formula is food cost divided by sales. Using the example, $10,000 divided by $40,000 is or 25%.
Answer B is wrong. The formula is food cost divided by sales. Using the example, $10,000 divided by 40,000 is or 25%.
Answer C is wrong. The formula is food cost divided by sales. Using the example, $10,000 divided by $40,000 is or 25%.
Answer D is wrong. The formula is food cost divided by sales. Using the example, $1,000 divided by $40,000 is or 25%.

Question #31
Answer A is wrong. The operating budget is not used in determining the hours of operation.
Answer B is wrong. The amount of vacation time a manager receives is not determined by the operating budget.
Answer C is correct. This purpose along with analyzing needs and measuring actual performance are important to the foodservice operation. Outlining goals and responsibilities is an important part of determining an operation's success.
Answer D is wrong. Retirement plans are not determined by the operating budget.

Question #32

Answer A is correct. Until money is deposited, it cannot be used or earn interest.

Answer B is wrong. Although this is important, this is not the key reason for securing and depositing funds as soon as possible.

Answer C is wrong. If clients are past due on accounts, they should be notified; however, this has nothing to do with securing and depositing the funds already obtained.

Answer D is wrong. Securing and depositing funds does not have anything to do with client relationships.

Question #33

Answer A is correct. Using these steps is important to help eliminate the risk of the capital budget being inadequate.

Answer B is wrong. Putting items on the list just because they are wanted and asking others for input does not provide adequate analysis of real need and could lead to unnecessary purchases.

Answer C is wrong. This process could lead to purchasing items that really are not needed and leave items that may be needed off the list.

Answer D is wrong. Vendors and customers should not be making decisions about the capital budget of the operation.

Question #34

Answer A is correct. By multiplying the number of customers for a time period and the average sale per customer, you can determine the sales forecast.

Answer B is wrong. Using only the drinks purchased will not provide an accurate sales forecast.

Answer C is wrong. This will only increase the value of sales.

Answer D is wrong. This will only increase the number of customers.

Question #35

Answer A is correct. Usually there are specific times established for bleeding a register. In addition the manager may bleed the register after busy periods.

Answer B is wrong. Bleeding the register is one of the manager's duties and should be done with great attention, therefore it should not be done when a manager needs a break.

Answer C is wrong. Bleeding the register should occur at the prescribed times which may not be at the end of their shift.

Answer D is wrong. The manager should bleed the register at the prescribed times and not just when they feel like doing it.

Question #36

Answer A is wrong. A business would need to know whether or not it can afford to remodel before scheduling the work to be done, but this is not determined by a profit and loss report.

Answer B is wrong. Customer satisfaction is not determined by a profit and loss statement, although, if sales are down, it may be a factor that needs to be investigated.

Answer C is correct. A profit and loss report is used to analyze trends and identify areas for improvement.

Answer D is wrong. The profit and loss report is not helpful in determining employee schedules.

Question #37

Answer A is correct. Controllable costs are those costs management can control by doing things such as changing recipes, using portion control, and pricing.

Answer B is wrong. Noncontrollable costs are things such as license fees or insurance fees over which management has no control.

Answer C is wrong. Fixed costs are costs that remain the same regardless of sales volume.

Answer D is wrong. Variable costs are costs that are based on sales.

Question #38
Answer A is wrong. Billing codes do not provide information regarding the account with which an item is associated.
Answer B is wrong. Item descriptions provide information about a specific item and not necessarily the account with which they are associated.
Answer C is correct. A chart of accounts provides categorical information that is used for accounting purposes in a business.
Answer D is wrong. Credit details do not provide any information about accounts.

Question #39
Answer A is wrong. This is the formula for dollars available for variable employees.
Answer B is wrong. This is an incorrect formula.
Answer C is wrong. The sales forecast must be multiplied by the standard labor cost percentage, not subtracted.
Answer D is correct. This calculation gives the amount of dollars that can be spent on labor costs for a given period. Benefits, deductions, and fixed labor costs must be subtracted before it can further be determined how much is available for hourly employees.

Question #40
Answer A is wrong. The formula is total sale per server divided by number of covers. Using the example, $800 divided by 40 is $20.
Answer B is wrong. The formula is total sale per server divided by number of covers. Using the example, $800 divided by 40 is $20.
Answer C is wrong. The formula is total sale per server divided by number of covers. Using the example, $800 divided by 40 is $20.
Answer D is correct. The formula is total sale per server divided by number of covers. Using the example, $800 divided by 40 is $20.

Question #41
Answer A is wrong. The payback period is the length of time it will take to recover the amount of an investment.
Answer B is wrong. FF&E are capital items.
Answer C is correct. This measurement helps to determine how much is saved or earned in the long run by making the purchase.
Answer D is wrong. Rate of return is the relationship between the savings or additional income and the amount spent on the item.

Question #42

Answer A is wrong. Profit and loss reports do not help with employee scheduling.

Answer B is correct. Differences are variances and could indicate problems that need resolution.

Answer C is wrong. Profit and loss reports do not help to determine how much sick time employees may have taken.

Answer D is wrong. Profit and loss reports to not analyze accountants to determine who may be better.

Question #43

Answer A is wrong. Credit limits typically refer to how much credit a person may receive.

Answer B is wrong. Amount owed is how much a person owes for goods or services received.

Answer C is correct. This describes the terms of credit and the payment rules.

Answer D is wrong. Balance is another term used to describe the amount owed, but not the terms.

Question #44

Answer A is wrong. The number of servers working does not determine how many meals a server can serve.

Answer B is wrong. The number of managers working does not determine how many meals a server can serve.

Answer C is correct. This standard is used to measure against sales forecast to determine the number of servers to schedule.

Answer D is wrong. The number of employees a manager can handle at one time does not help determine how many meals a server can serve.

Question #45

Answer A is wrong. Rate of return is the relationship between the savings or additional income and the amount spent on the item.
Answer B is correct. The payback period is the length of time it will take to recover the amount of an investment. Generally speaking, the shorter the period to recover the funds spent on an item, the better the investment is.
Answer C is wrong. The return on investment is a measurement of the financial benefits of a purchase.
Answer D is wrong. The operating budget is used for daily operations and not for long term major purchases.

Question #46

Answer A is wrong. Monitoring the budget is not the same as watching every line of the budget while looking for differences.
Answer B is correct. By comparing line items, specific differences can be analyzed.
Answer C is wrong. A sales review does not analyze line items.
Answer D is wrong. An audit may include a line item review but should include other analysis also.

Question #47

Answer A is wrong. Overages may show on the reports, but management needs to look for variances so possible problems can be caught.
Answer B is wrong. Under runs do not help to analyze possible problems.
Answer C is wrong. This comparison will not help to determine efficiency.
Answer D is correct. Variances help to prevent future problems by catching them early.

Question #48
Answer A is wrong. This would keep an employee from using the cash presented as evidence if a situation should arise regarding the amount of cash presented.

Answer B is correct. This will eliminate questions regarding the amount of cash presented by the customer.

Answer C is wrong. The customer should not be asked to hold his payment until change can be given.

Answer D is wrong. Change should be counted and the cash presented should not be placed in the register drawer until it is counted.

Question #49
Answer A is wrong. Usually only managers or finance employees know when bills should be paid.

Answer B is wrong. Employees, regardless of their popularity, are not necessarily informed well enough to make the decision of when to pay bills.

Answer C is wrong. Vendors should not decide the finances of the business.

Answer D is correct. The person paying invoices should be aware of the budget of the business as well as the current financial status.

Question #50
Answer A is wrong. Fixed costs do not vary. The manager's salary is fixed, but the server's salary is variable.

Answer B is wrong. Variable costs change in direct proportion to sales volumes. The server's salary is variable, but the manager's salary is fixed regardless of sales volume.

Answer C is correct. Variable costs are made up of both fixed and variable costs. Labor costs fall into this category.

Answer D is wrong. Management can control salaries.

Managerial Accounting Glossary

Account code   unique number assigned to each of the individual category accounts listed on an operation's chart of accounts

Accounts payable   amount of money owed by an operation to others (such as suppliers of food and beverage products and other services)

Accounts receivable   money owed to the operation by its customers and clients

Aging schedule   chart that shows the amount and length of time individual accounts receivable have been owed to the operation

Bleed   process of removing cash from a cash register during a shift for the purpose of storing that cash more securely

Capital budget   spending plan for major purchases of items that will be used over a long period of time

Capital item   same as furnishings, fixtures, and equipment (FF&E). Typically the life of a capital item is in excess of one year

Chart of accounts   list of categories used to separate an operation's expense information

Controllable cost   cost that managers can directly control

Corrective action   steps taken to remedy a cost control problem

Cost/benefit analysis   process of evaluating the purchase price (cost) of an item relative to the cost savings achieved by owning the item

Cover   one customer meal

Covers per server   number of customers that a server can serve in one hour

Credit terms   payment rules developed for those customers who are allowed to establish house accounts

Depreciation   method of calculating and recording the reduction in the value of an asset over its useful lifetime

Economy study   direct financial comparison of the cost/ benefit analysis of two or more alternatives

Fixed cost   cost that remains the same regardless of variations in sales volume

Food cost   actual dollar value of the food used during a specific accounting period

Food cost percentage   ratio that measures the relationship between sales and the cost of the food needed to generate the sales

Food product waste   measure of the amount of food taken from inventory but not actually sold

Forecast   prediction of sales levels or costs that will occur during a specific time period

Furnishings, fixtures, and equipment (FF&E)   items purchased with funds designated in a capital budget

Gratuity   amount of money freely given by a guest as a reward for good service. Also known as a "tip."

Income statement   a valuable management tool. Also known as a "profit and loss report."

Invoice   vendor's sales document that lists details such as items purchased, date of order, purchaser, and sales price(s)

Labor cost   employee wages and all other directly related payroll costs, such as the employer's contribution to FICA and Medicare, workers' compensation insurance, and employee benefits

Labor cost percentage   ratio of labor cost to revenue (Labor cost ÷ Sales revenue = Labor cost percentage)

Line item review   process of checking budgeted amounts against actual results obtained for each category listed in a budget

Loss   if sales are lower than costs, the operation shows a loss

Master schedule   spreadsheet showing the number of people needed in each position to run the foodservice operation

Moving average   average calculated from two or more recent and similar accounting periods

Noncontrollable cost   cost over which managers have little or no direct control

Operating budget   projected financial plan for a specific period of time

Payback period   length of time it will take to pay back an investment

Payroll costs   amount of money spent for fixed and variable employee wages

Profit   if sales are higher than costs, the operation is making a profit

Profit and loss report   a compilation of sales and cost information for a specific period of time. This report shows whether an operation has made or lost money during the time period covered

Rate of return   relationship between the savings (or additional income) achieved by purchasing an item, and the amount spent on the item

Reconciliation   to check one number against another for accuracy

Return on investment   ratio that measures the amount of increase in invested money over a specific period of time. Also know as "ROI."

Sales   includes all of the income made in the given time period covered by the profit and loss report

Security feature   physical characteristic of currency that helps to deter counterfeiters. Examples include portraits and watermarks

Semivariable cost   cost that will increase and decrease, respectively, as sales increase and decrease, but not in direct proportion

Standard   amount of cost that management has determined is appropriate

Subtotal   sum of the selling prices of the individual menu items listed on a guest check; also, the total amount due for a guest check prior to the addition of taxes and/or gratuities

Variable cost   cost that should increase and decrease in direct proportion to sales

Variance   difference between two (usually numeric) values. Variance may be expressed as a percentage or as an absolute numeric difference

Voucher   numbered form that allows for the recording of invoice payment information